An Elizabethan Christmas

The fourth title in the Elizabethan Needlework series
and the second by Sheila Marshall

by Sheila Marshall

PUBLISHER'S NOTE

The designs in this book were made using fabric, threads and general supplies available in retail shops in New Zealand. As publisher, we are aware that some of these items may not be found in your local shop, so every effort has been made to include and suggest alternative materials that can be found in specialist needlework retailers in your country. We believe and know that the alternatives suggested will give very satisfactory results, and most importantly in the end, a beautiful set of Christmas Decorations to be enjoyed for many Christmases to come! As always we welcome your letters, email messages and telephone calls. The messages we receive from everywhere needlework is enjoyed brighten our day! Please let us know how you progress through this book.

Prue Georgeson

Published by Georgeson Publishing Limited
P.O. Box 100-667, North Shore Mail Centre, New Zealand 1330.
Ph: 649 410 2079 Fax: 649 410 2069
Email: gpl@georgeson.co.nz Web site: www.georgeson.co.nz

ISBN 0-9582105-2-7

Editor: Prue Georgeson
Photography: Maria Sainsbury
Illustrations and Layout: Andreena Buckton of Noodle Design Corp.
Printed: Hong Kong

Contents

ELIZABETHAN STYLE CHRISTMAS TREE DECORATIONS
INTRODUCTION

Christmas is a season that is eagerly anticipated by most of us. Buying presents, wrapping and posting them when required, decorating the Christmas tree and our homes, planning meals and cooking food. Many of these activities were also carried out by our 16th century forebears.

In Elizabethan times gifts were exchanged at New Year rather than Christmas and the range of gifts received by Elizabeth I is extremely varied. Beautifully embroidered cushions, books presented with richly embroidered covers, gloves made of doeskin with coloured silk embroidery cuffs, are just some of the gifts recorded.

Each of the twelve decorations featured in this book has been inspired by the life and times of the Elizabethans. They have been designed to fit into the modern home and are made with stitch techniques from the past but using fabrics, threads and braids freely available now. The stitches and construction techniques used are all explained clearly at the front of this book.

They are fun to make and very satisfying. I made mine using scraps of fabric saved from previous projects. I have a hoard of favourite bits and pieces that I have kept 'knowing' they would be useful at some future date. Most embroiderers seem to have a similar hoard!

The designs on the front of each decoration are worked in three different methods, two in needle lace, four in raised work, the rest in applique. They all have the same motif, a holly leaf and berries, on the back. Gold braid of various weights and beads have been used to create the rich, rather luscious look of Elizabethan Embroidery.

While lists of requirements and stitching details are given with each decoration you may wish to use your own choice of fabrics and colours. Make all twelve decorations or just make the individual designs. What a special Christmas gift these would make for a treasured friend! Gather together all the materials and prepare the pieces for each decoration before you begin the stitching (the fun part) and you will achieve the results much more quickly than if you have to stop to find things, cut up fabric shapes and so on.

Have a happy time.

Sheila Marshall.

ELIZABETHAN NOTES

Elizabethan Embroidery in the 16th century flourished as it is flourishing again now with renewed interest in this colourful and textured embroidery.

The sixteenth century was a time of peace and prosperity with increased wealth particularly in the middle and upper classes. The associated rise in living standards was reflected in increased enrichment of their clothing and increased decoration within their homes.

The embroidery from this period is magnificent. The needlewomen and professional embroiderers had a repertoire of stitches we could all envy and emulate! Inspiration for their stitching was all around them in the newly fashionable flower gardens and patterns and drawings for these flowers were becoming more available with the arrival of the first pattern books. The improved quality of the steel needles that became available was a further impetus to the 'flowering' of beautiful stitching from this period.

Coloured silk embroidery was one of three types of embroidery which were very popular in this period, along with Blackwork and whitework, consisting of drawn threadwork fillings and reticella motifs. Coloured silk embroidery is inspiring embroiderers again and *The Elizabethan Needlework Series* (of which *An Elizabethan Christmas* is the fourth title in the series) have been produced to encourage and teach modern needlewomen. The embroidery in these books has been inspired by the work from the past but recreated using fabric and threads available today.

Exploring Elizabethan Embroidery by Dorothy Clarke serves as an introduction to this embroidery. Colourful and textured the designs in this book introduce you to the stitches and techniques used with clear, easy-to-follow stitch diagrams and instructions. Start a delightful journey of discovery!

Elizabethan Needlework Accessories by Sheila Marshall extends your knowledge of embroidery techniques used in the Elizabethan period. The embroidery is worked on a variety of different fabrics and the range of designs will delight the embroiderer. The 'Petal Hussif' has been stitched and acclaimed world wide.

Festive Elizabethan Creations by Shirley Holdaway features designs for the special occasions in our lives. The Juliet Bride's Cap and Bag won 'Best of Show' at the prestigious Woodlawn Plantation Exhibition at Virginia in USA and delights all who see it. Shirley shares with us her techniques for creating stunning three dimensional flowers. This is embroidery for the enthusiast.

An Elizabethan Christmas by Sheila Marshall is a further book in the series introducing more stitch techniques, all illustrated in easy-to-follow diagrams with clear supporting text. These decorations will be a delight to the eye for years to come and part of the special magic of Christmas at your home.

We plan further titles in this series. They will provide a chance for you to develop a stitch repertoire of Elizabethan proportions!

Necessities

Satin Fabric

To give a rich and decorative look to this embroidery it has been worked on satin which combines well with the couched gold threads and embroidery. The satin is always 'backed' with a fine cotton fabric so that the fabric does not 'pull' with the embroidery on the surface. Silk or rayon would be suitable alternative fabrics to use with a sheen, a closely woven linen could also be used.

Backing Fabric

The backing fabric gives strength to your embroidery and is a most useful extra layer to start and finish threads where they will not be seen. All the embroidery in this book is 'backed' before the gold threads are couched on, or further stitching is worked. To 'back' lay the main fabric on top of the backing very carefully, smooth out the wrinkles and then put into the frame together, stretching tightly. *Do not* stitch the backing and main fabric together as they often pull in different directions when put in the frame.

Other Materials

- Bonding Web comes in two weights. Both weights are suitable for use in these designs and will give a most pleasing end result. The lighter weight is possibly a little easier to sew through, than the heavier, which I used.
- Heavy Duty Vilene is used for making bags etc, it can be seen through to trace shapes and several layers can be used to build up thickness. It doesn't fray which is another very useful attribute!
- Contact and calico are used when creating needlelace or punto in aria. The contact plastic adheres to the calico and creates a 'fabric' not unlike the parchment used for this purpose by the Elizabethans.
- Ironing cloth - It is wise to use a piece of cotton fabric between the iron and the satin when ironing on the Bonding web as this not only protects the satin, but seems to prevent pencil lines smudging or spreading.
- Tracing paper used in needlelace.
- 30 gauge white covered wire (bought in embroidery shops), good quality white covered cake wire is the same. Alternatively 28 gauge uncovered wire can be used. (A slightly heavier uncovered wire is used as a 30 gauge uncovered wire is too fine to keep a shape.)
- fine clutch pencil (0.5mm lead) - when tracing the small, fine designs in this book it is important to use a fine tipped pencil so the traced design only marks the satin lightly.

Threads

DMC rayon threads are the main threads that have been used in this embroidery as the sheen of these threads goes well with the satin fabric and couched gold threads. (In the thread tables we give the DMC rayon number (remove the first 3 or 30 and you have the correct stranded cotton number). Silk and stranded cottons could also be used and alternative threads are given in the tables. One strand of rayon equals two threads of stranded cotton or silk, if you prefer to use these. Gold coloured sewing cotton is used for couching the gold thread and cord. Cream sewing cotton is used for sewing the decorations together.

Gold Threads and Cords
In keeping with the 'lush' appearance of Elizabethan embroidery, gold threads and fine gold cords have been used extensively in these decorations. These are couched in position and full instructions for doing this are given in the stitch section. I have used different weights of thread and gold cord which I specify in the tables, if you can't get the particular threads mentioned, *buy whatever is available in your favourite needlework shop of the correct weight.*

Needles
Crewel Needles Sizes 3 and 10 are used with the rayon or stranded cottons and silk and the fine metallic gold thread. Tapestry Sizes 24 or 26 are used for the needle lace. A large eyed darning needle may be useful when couching for taking the heavier gold cords to the back of the fabric. Beading Needle Size 10 may be necessary for sewing on the beads (sometimes the fine crewel can be used) and also a Sharp sewing needle Size 9 for couching and construction.

Beads
Beads have been used on the Christmas Decorations to enrich their appearance and add highlights. They have been grouped to form grapes, or flowers and used individually to represent jewels. The main beads used are seed beads with the occasional larger bead specified for example on the 'crown' of the falcon.

Scissors
Three different types of scissors are needed. A pair of kitchen scissors for cutting out the cardboard, dressmakers scissors for cutting out the fabric and a little pair of embroidery scissors for cutting threads.

Embroidery Frame
An embroidery frame is *absolutely essential* for this embroidery. Threads cannot be couched in position unless the fabric to be worked is held firmly. A 10 cm (4") round frame is ideal for these decorations. If your frame is too large for your embroidery, take a larger piece of backing fabric which does fit your frame, stretch it tightly into the frame and then tack your main fabric piece onto the backing material in the frame. When using a hoop frame, tighten the screw very firmly with a screw driver.

TRANSFERRING THE DESIGN

There are many different ways of transferring designs to fabric. In this embroidery it is made easier as the designs are mainly transferred to satins which can be seen through, making tracing easy. You may trace just the outlines or include couching lines also. The couching lines, if traced finely, will be hidden by the fine gold metallic thread. When using the darker satins for example the 'swete bag' you may find the use of a Light Box or Sewing Carbon Paper helpful. Another alternative is to trace the design shape onto heavy duty vilene cut this out and use as a template. More detailed information on these different methods is given. Detailed instructions are given with each decoration.

TRACING THE DESIGN

Most of the designs are transferred on to light coloured satin so it is easy to trace the design from the book to the fabric. I use a fine lead (0.5mm) pencil such as one of the 'clutch' or propelling drawing pencils that are cheaply available. These work well as they do not smudge or become messy, making your threads dirty, as do conventional pencils. *Avoid making any more marks than are absolutely necessary and use the pencil lightly.*

THE LIGHT BOX METHOD

Place the design to be traced on the glass. Position the design on your fabric with care and trace the design. If you do not have a light box there are alternatives. Photocopy the design, darken with a black felt tip pen, tape it to your window and then tape the fabric over the top of the design and trace. Or use a glass table with a lamp underneath it to create light box conditions.

SEWING CARBON PAPER

This technique may be useful with the Swete Bag, Undress Hat and Book which are worked on darker fabric. Trace the design from the book onto paper. Then place a piece of sewing carbon paper on top of your fabric, place the design on top of that. Trace the design onto your fabric with a fine tip (preferably used up) ball point pen or something similar.

TEMPLATE METHOD

This gives the outline of the shape only but is a useful technique to use at different times. Trace the outline on to heavy duty vilene, cut out the shape and use this as a template. Or trace the outline on to tracing paper, stick the tracing paper onto cardboard, cut out the shape and use this as a template.

FISHBONE STITCH
ALSO CALLED LEAF SATIN

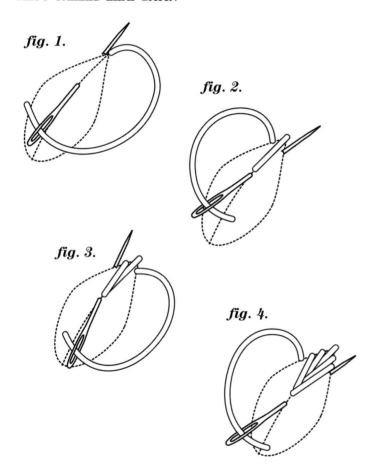

fig. 1.

fig. 2.

fig. 3.

fig. 4.

Fishbone stitch gives a nice smooth appearance to your embroidery. I find it a most useful stitch as it is easier to do neatly than satin stitch but gives the same effect. It is stitched using a Crewel size 9 or 10 needle.

To start bring the thread through at the tip of the leaf and make a straight stitch approximately a third of the length of the shape to be filled along the centre line of the shape (fig. 1).

Bring the thread through again to the left of the thread at the tip of the leaf and make a sloping stitch taking the needle down at the centre just below the point where the first stitch finished (fig. 2). Bring the thread through at the right of the first stitch and make a similar sloping stitch (fig. 3).

Continue working alternately on each side until the shape is filled (fig. 4). Stitches should be worked closely together.

SATIN STITCH

Satin stitch is used to great effect in many different styles of embroidery. Stitch using a Crewel Size 9 or 10 needle.

This stitch should be worked with close even stitches to cover the fabric completely. Work the stitches on an angle across the area outlined and do not make the stitches too long or pull too tightly. It is easier to achieve a nice angle to your stitching if you start in the middle of the shape (fig. 1) and work to fill one side. Return to the centre and work in the opposite direction to fill the other side (fig. 2).

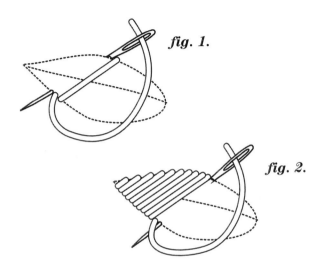

fig. 1.

fig. 2.

CHAIN STITCH

Chain stitch is used extensively in Elizabethan Embroidery.

It is frequently used as an outline for shapes into which further stitches are worked. In the embroidery in this book single chains are used to create small flowers and a decorative pattern on the cuff of the glove.

Single chains are created by working a basic chain stitch (fig. 1). The needle is then taken to the back of the fabric at the end of the stitch to anchor it and brought to the front in the correct position to work the next stitch. (fig. 2). It is best stitched with a Crewel Size 9 or 10 needle.

Single chains can be grouped to make an attractive, simple flower or arranged to create a leaf pattern. It is a stitch with lots of possibilities!

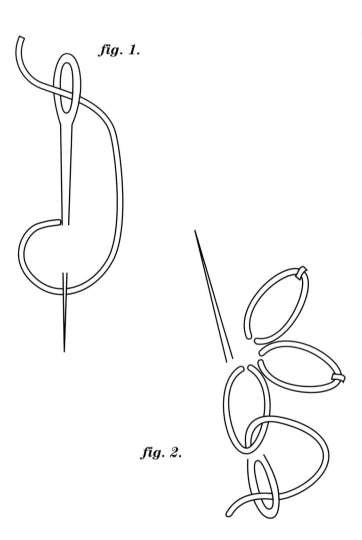

fig. 1.

fig. 2.

FLY STITCH

Fly stitch is a most useful filling stitch. It can be stitched in patterns, arranged to create heavy or light fillings or just 'scattered' over an area to give texture and depth as it is on the eagle.

Bring the thread to the surface at the left (A), hold the thread down with your left thumb insert the needle at (B) bringing it out at (C) as shown in fig. 1. Take a short or long stitch over the 'v' to anchor it, (fig. 2). The length of the straight stitch anchoring the 'v' can be varied depending on the effect you are wishing to achieve. It is best stitched with a Crewel Size 9 or 10 needle.

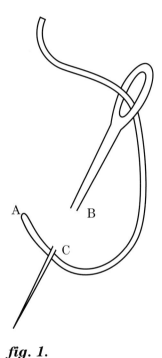

fig. 1.

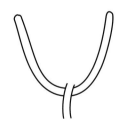

fig. 2.

COUCHING

Metallic thread was used frequently in Elizabethan times and it has been used extensively in these Christmas Decorations. It is best couched in place. When couching it is common to use threads of a heavier weight than those used elsewhere in the embroidery. To bring these threads to the surface thread them through the eye of a Size 3 Crewel needle or a large-eyed darning needle.

In couching two threads are used, the thread to be couched (laid) and the 'couching thread' which is stitched over the *laid* thread to hold the *laid* thread in the correct position and attach it to the fabric.

All this embroidery is worked on backed fabrics so that the metallic threads can be secured at the beginning and end into the backing and these stitches will be completely invisible on the top of the work.

To couch your embroidery it must be held firmly in a frame.

I start couching in different places depending on the particular shape to be couched round, I usually start at the base of the leaf or petal or at one end of a line or shape. When couching round shapes like the Knight or Boot, it is best to choose a place to begin where one line joins another so that the starting and finishing is not very noticeable. *Never begin or finish in the middle of a line.*

When couching designs that are small like these with lots of short lines reasonably close together, do not cut the gold 'laid' thread and start again. Rather take the thread down at the end of the line, carry it across the back of the work and come to the front at the start of the next line, as long as the distance between the end of one line and the start of the next is not too great.

When working curls or scrolls, begin at the main stem and go down at the centre of the curl, this makes it easier to make a nicely shaped curl.

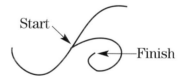

Place your laid thread where you wish to being stitching then take the laid thread end to the back of your work using the large eyed needle (fig. 1).

At the back of your work fasten the laid thread end securely into the backing using your couching thread (sewing cotton threaded in a sharp pointed needle) and stitch firmly. Next bring the couching thread through to the front on the line to be couched 6 mm (1/4") from the start and directly beneath the laid thread (fig. 2). Remember to work from right to left. Take the couching thread over the laid thread and return back down through the fabric in the same position that you came up, actually *under* the laid thread (fig. 3). This makes the thread fit snugly round the laid thread and holds it firmly in place. All stitches are worked in a 'stab' fashion.

Continue couching the laid thread along the design line holding the laid thread in position with one hand and working couching stitches 6mm (1/4") apart (fig. 4). Remember to keep a little tension on the laid line. Sometimes with very small designs the couching stitches may need to be closer together.When you are nearly at the end of the design line take your laid thread through to the back of your fabric before completing the last few couching stitches. Complete the last couching stitches then take the couching thread to the back and sew down the end of the laid thread and finish off. I neaten my beginnings and endings as I go. This is not the traditional method but it does avoid any tangles under or on top of my work!

You will need to work the couching stitches more closely together when taking the laid thread around curves. When working round points always have a stitch at the tip and a stitch close to the tip on each side (fig. 5).

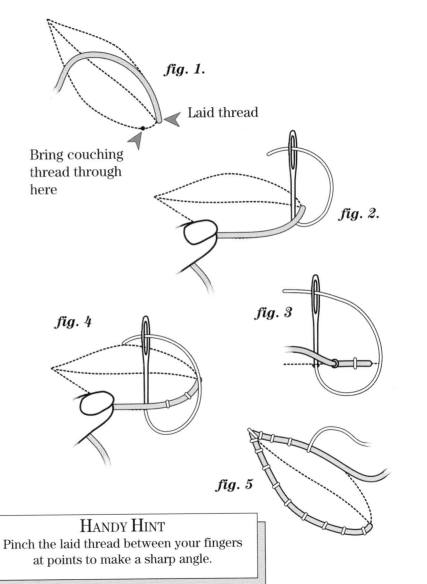

fig. 1.

Laid thread

Bring couching thread through here

fig. 2.

fig. 3

fig. 4

fig. 5

HANDY HINT
Pinch the laid thread between your fingers
at points to make a sharp angle.

LONG BULLION STITCH

This stitch is not an Elizabethan stitch but it is a most useful stitch technique when working on a small scale. Bullions are usually worked with the needle pointing upwards (or upwards and left) as this makes it easier to wind the many wraps required and also to hold the wraps on the needle.

Bring the needle out at B and take a small stitch 2 mm (1/8") at the centre of the flower, A - B (fig. 1). Do not pull the needle out of the fabric but with the eye of the needle still in the fabric hold the fabric so that the needle is pointing upwards and is perpendicular to the material. Wrap the thread (single strand of DMC rayon) loosely around the needle in a clockwise direction 22 times, do not overlap the wraps (fig. 2).

Gently holding the wraps on the needle pull the needle and thread though the wraps carefully. Once the needle is through, spread the wraps evenly along the thread then keep pulling the thread until it is tight and smooth.

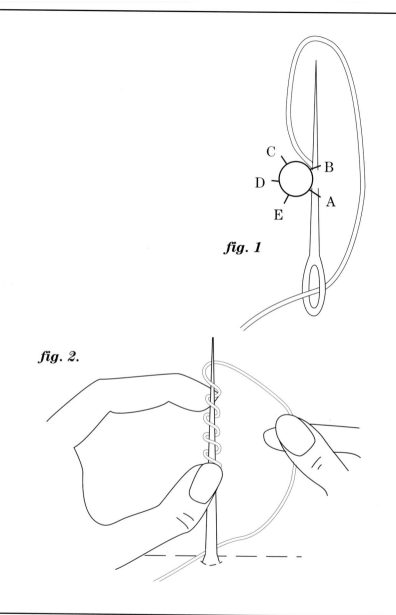

fig. 1

fig. 2.

HANDY HINT
Before starting bullions make sure the thread is not already twisted by letting the needle hang freely to allow the thread to untwist.

If the bullion gets lumpy before taking the needle through to the back of the fabric, slide the needle under and lift it from the fabric. Work the needle back and forth and keep pulling on the thread (fig. 3). Or spread the wraps out, loosen and rearrange them along the thread, then pull thread tight before taking needle to back of work

Take the needle to the back of the fabric at A, pull through really tightly before securing by doing a little back stitch at the back of the work (fig. 4). This helps to keep the loop in front in place and also prevents twisting.

Bring needle to the surface and repeat between C - B, D - C, E - D and A - E The flower is worked in an anti clockwise direction.

Work another circle of bullions on top of the one already worked as shown. They are worked between the petals of the bottom row in the same way (fig. 5).

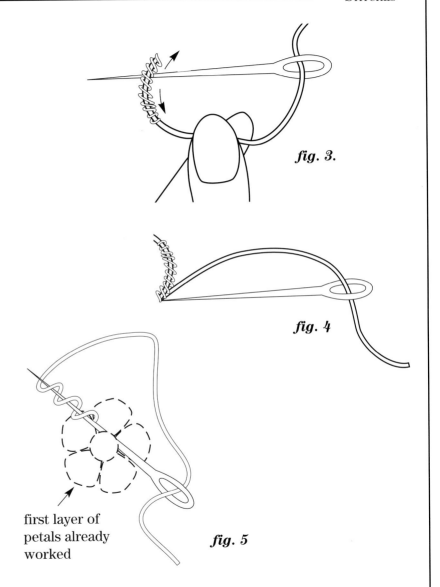

fig. 3.

fig. 4

first layer of petals already worked

fig. 5

HANDY HINT
If loops twist no matter what your stitch tension may not need so many wraps so try doing 19, or whatever works for the particular size you need. It is common for different people to achieve the same good result by using more or less wraps. Practice really does make perfect!

PUNTO IN ARIA
ALSO CALLED NEEDLE LACE

Punto in Aria or needle lace has been used to create the free standing petals in the Eglantine Rose and the wings of the butterfly. The foundation thread may be doubled thread or wire and as I wanted the petals and butterfly to be three dimensional I used wire as this will sit 'forward' even after years of use.

These instructions cover the preparations for, and couching of wire round different shapes. The instructions for stitching the butterfly are given on page 32 and the instructions for the rose are on page 29.

YOU WILL NEED
- Calico scraps - two pieces for backing - they only need to be a little larger than the design of the shape to be stitched
- Tracing paper and pencil
- Contact
- Sewing cotton for couching, to match embroidery thread
- Sharp needle for sewing cotton used in couching
- White covered 30 gauge wire see page 27 for alternatives

PREPARATION
Trace the shapes to be worked onto tracing paper, lay the tracing on top of the two pieces of calico which have been tacked together and then cover the tracing paper with contact.

The two layers of calico give a firm surface to work on and make it easy to cut and unpick the couching stitches after you have made the needle lace. You will find the contact adheres to the calico very well. An embroidery frame is not necessary, but may be used if you prefer (fig. 1).

HANDY HINT
Use wire snips or old scissors to cut the wire.

To begin, thread a sharp sewing needle with sewing cotton that matches your subsequent needle lace filling (double for strength). You will use this to couch the foundation wire in place. This thread should match the subsequent needle lace filling so that if you do not manage to pull all the little couching stitches out any stray threads won't show. If the subsequent needle lace filling has more than one colour use one thread that blends with all the colours to be used.

Anchor this couching thread (sewing cotton) very firmly at the back in the calico with a couple of back stitches. Then bring the couching thread to the surface, at the base of the petal, bend the wire round the point and couch the wire in position leaving enough space for the needle to go between the couching stitches comfortably when the needle lace is being worked (fig. 2).

Couch the foundation wire round all the lines on the needle lace shape to be filled, overlapping the wire at the start and finish. Treat the wire like thread, lay it on the shape and stitch in place as you go, bending to follow the curves in the outline as you come to them. You will find the wire very pliable and easy to bend to the right shape.

To finish off your couching thread, take it to the back of your work and secure firmly with a couple of back stitches into the calico.

Following the appropriate stitch instructions work the filling stitches. When the filling is complete and you wish to remove your embroidery from the calico, undo the tacking stitches holding the two layers of calico together then pull these two layers of calico apart and cut the couching stitches. This way there is no chance of cutting your embroidery as there are only one set of threads to see - those to be cut.

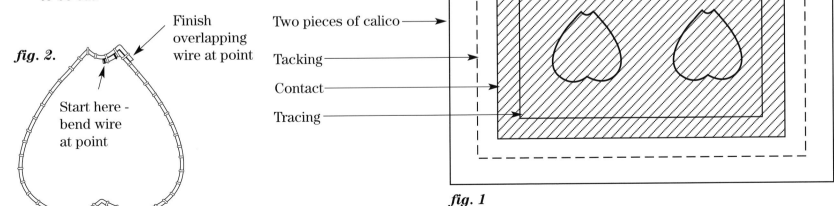

fig. 2.

Finish overlapping wire at point

Start here - bend wire at point

Two pieces of calico

Tacking

Contact

Tracing

fig. 1

DETACHED BUTTONHOLE

ALSO KNOWN AS CORDED BUTTONHOLE
used for Rose petals

Detached buttonhole stitch is used extensively in
Elizabethan embroidery. It can be worked directly onto the
material (see earlier books in the Elizabethan Needlework
Series) or worked as it is in this book as a filling stitch in
needle lace.

Detached buttonhole stitch is worked in one direction - from
left to right. The thread is returned from right to left with a
long straight stitch.

TO START

Using a tapestry needle run the thread up through the
couching threads to the starting point. Wrap the thread
around the wire foundation on the left hand side as shown
(fig. 1).

Then work detached buttonhole stitch across the tip to the
other side, you will only work about three stitches. Do not
make the stitches too tight as the needle will need to go
between these stitches easily when working the next row.

At the right hand side wrap the thread you are stitching with
twice round the foundation thread, (one wrap to anchor and
one wrap to cover) before looping it across to the left hand
side where you catch the thread around the wire foundation
twice on this side also. Now continue working detached

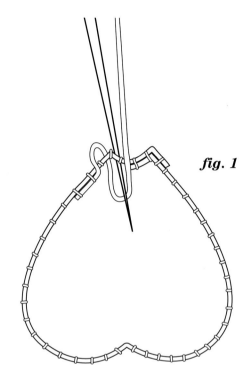

fig. 1

HANDY HINT
As this is quite fine embroidery you may find you prefer
to just wrap the thread around the wire once each side.

buttonhole stitch into each loop of the stitch above and catching the straight thread underneath as well (fig. 2). Repeat this until the area is filled. When you reach the point where the petal divides into two shapes, these two spaces are worked separately (fig. 3).

When you are working detached buttonhole stitch filling you must wrap the thread over the wire at the end of each row and the beginning of the next to attach the stitching to the foundation, keeping it altogether.

To Finish

To finish run the thread along through a few of the wraps that cover the foundation thread, as you did when starting.

Starting and Finishing Threads in the Middle of a Shape

When you wish to finish a thread in the middle of a needle lace shape, this may be done either at the end of a row of detached buttonhole stitch or after the bar has been laid back across the work. Start and finish new threads in the same way as described under 'To Start' and 'To Finish'.

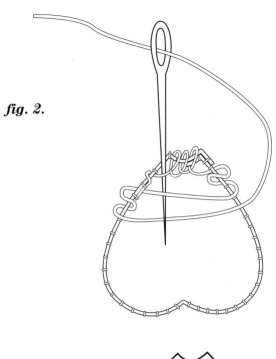

fig. 2.

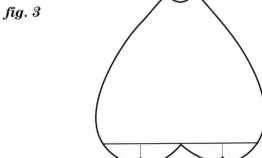

fig. 3

Increasing and Decreasing

To create an attractively shaped petal you will need to increase and decrease at times. This is easily accomplished. When you wish to increase just work extra buttonhole stitches at the intervals where required along the row you are stitching (fig. 4). When you wish to decrease, just work less stitches along the row (fig. 5).

Buttonhole Edging

When the petal has been completely filled with detached buttonhole stitch buttonhole right round the edge. This ensures your wire is completely hidden as well as catching in any finishing threads very securely. It also makes a very attractive edge for the decorations. To start the buttonhole edge - do this at a different point to where you started couching so that you avoid 'bulk' at any one point, run the thread through wraps round the wire, finish in the same way. I used fine gold metallic thread to give added richness to my petals but a different coloured stranded cotton could be used if you prefer (fig. 6).

Removing the Petal from the Calico

To lift the petal away from the calico when the filling is complete, undo the tacking stitches holding the two layers of calico together then pull these two layers of calico apart and cut the couching stitches. This way there is no chance of cutting your embroidery as there are only one set of threads to see - those to be cut. Pull out any loose couching threads with tweezers and your petal is ready to be attached to the flower base.

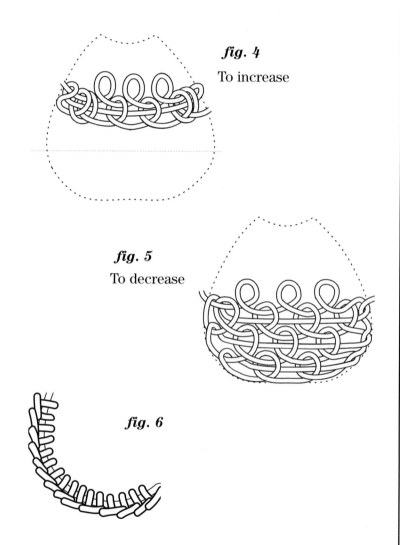

fig. 4
To increase

fig. 5
To decrease

fig. 6

SINGLE BRUSSELS STITCH

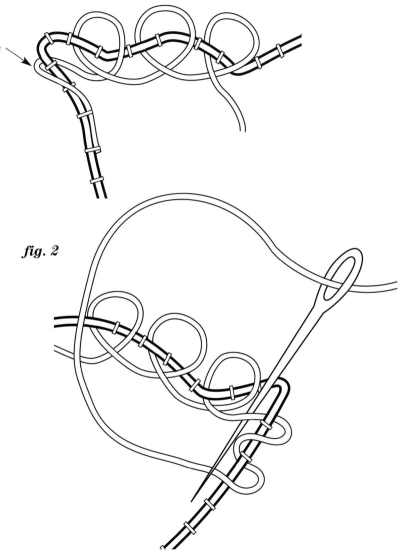

fig. 1
Start here

Single Brussels stitch is a much used stitch, it is also called detached buttonhole stitch and open buttonhole filling stitch. Really it is just a simple detached buttonhole stitch. It is used in many different stitch techniques and seems to have acquired a variety of names so don't be put off by a different name it is really only a minor variation on buttonhole stitch.

In this book single Brussels stitch is used in needle lace. It is worked from left to right, then anchored at the end of each row by wrapping the thread twice around the wire foundation before being worked back across the shape from right to left.

fig. 2

TO START
Using a tapestry needle, run the thread up through the couching threads to the starting point indicated on fig 1. Then buttonhole stitch across the wire foundation to the other side. Do not make the stitches too tight as the needle will need to go between these stitches easily when working the next row.

At the right hand side wrap the thread you are stitching with twice round the foundation thread. (One wrap to anchor and one wrap to cover.) Now work back across the row from right to left by working buttonhole stitches into the stitches in the row above (fig. 2).

Once back at the left hand side wrap the thread twice round the foundation thread as you did on the right hand side then buttonhole back across the petals. Repeat the last two rows back and forth until the section is filled. Increase and decrease as required.

TO INCREASE

At times you will need to increase or decrease to ensure your stitches cover the shape. To increase, work two buttonhole stitches into one loop. This can be done at the beginning and end of a row or through the row if required (fig. 3).

TO DECREASE

To reduce the width of your shape you must reduce the number of stitches worked in each row. To do this work the first stitch into the second loop of the row above rather than the first, you may want to miss a loop or loops in the middle of the row also (fig. 4).

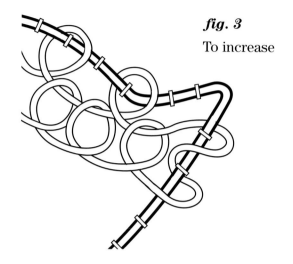

fig. 3

To increase

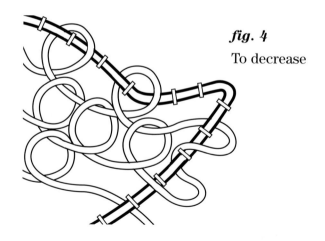

fig. 4

To decrease

STARTING AND FINISHING THREADS IN THE MIDDLE OF A SHAPE

The butterfly has multi-coloured wings stitched in four different colours. A new colour may be introduced at either end of your stitching (just not mid row!).
Start and finish new threads as described under 'To Start' and 'To Finish'.

TO FINISH

To finish run the thread along through a few of the wraps that cover the foundation thread, as you did when starting.

BUTTONHOLE EDGING

When the wings have been completely filled with detached buttonhole stitch, buttonhole right round the edge. This ensures your wire is completely hidden as well as catching in any finishing threads very securely. It also makes a very attractive edge for the decorations. To start the buttonhole edge - do this at a different point to where you started couching so that you avoid 'bulk' at any one point, run the thread through wraps round the wire, finish in the same way. I used fine gold metallic thread to give added richness to my wings but if you prefer a different coloured stranded cotton could be used (fig. 5).

REMOVING THE WINGS FROM THE CALICO

To lift the wings away from the calico when the filling is complete, undo the tacking stitches holding the two layers of calico together then pull these two layers of calico apart and cut the couching stitches. This way there is no chance of cutting your embroidery as there are only one set of threads to see - those to be cut. Pull out any loose couching threads with tweezers and your wings are ready to be attached to the satin.

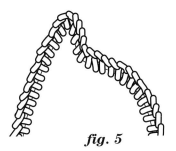

fig. 5

HANDY HINT
As this is quite fine embroidery you may find you prefer to just wrap the thread around the wire once each side

REQUIREMENTS

Cardboard 30 x 40 cm (12 x 16 inch) piece of cardboard, the backs of writing pads are ideal for use as the back of each decoration

12 x 9 cm (3 1/2") diameter PVC plastic flanges use for fronts, obtainable from plumbing supply shops. (These give a raised shape and allow space for the bulk of the gathering when laced fronts and backs are stitched together.) Alternatively use cardboard, an extra 30 x 40 cm (12 x 16 inch) piece required.

Heavy duty Vilene 30 x 90 cm (12 x 36") If cardboard is used for the front of each decoration rather than the flanges, additional vilene will be required for padding 15 x 90 cm (6 x 36").

Gold satin background fabric 60cm (24")

Backing Fabric (fine cotton) 1m (1 yard)

Bonding Web 25 x 40 cm (10 x 16")

Contact 10cm (4") square

Calico two 15cm (6") squares

Tracing paper

Fine clutch pencil 0.5mm lead

Dark green satin 20 cm (8") square for holly leaves

Variety of different coloured satin 10 cm (4") squares for use in Decorations: wine, red, peacock, royal blue, crushed strawberry, blue, brown, light green, cream, white and fawn, or colours of your choice. Specific requirements are given with each design.

Sewing cotton - cream and gold coloured for couching (Mettler colour 767, Gutermann 968 or any good matching thread.)

Fine gold metallic thread DMC 282 fine thread used in couching

Craft metallic gold 1 mm x 4 metres (1/32" x 4 yards) heavier thread used in couching

Crinkle metallic gold 20 cms (8") used in 'Swete Bag' for handle

Craft metallic "heavy" 2 mm x 2 m (1/16" x 2yd) gold cord (for hanging loop on decorations)

Gold metallic braid 3mm x 25 cm (3/16" x 10") used on cushion

Gold metallic braid 6 mm x 4 metres (1/4inch x 4 yards) used round edge of all decorations

Red beads 1 mm (120 over all) 10 each decoration

Glue stick (All metallic threads braids etc will be easier to use if a touch of the glue stick is wiped across the ends before threading in needle or using.)

Needles: Crewel needles sizes 10 and 3 (for thicker metallic threads), Tapestry needles size 24 (for needle lace), Beading Needle Size 10 for attaching beads, Sharps Size 9 for construction.

Double sided tape

10 cm embroidery hoop

30 gauge white covered wire, fine craft wire or covered cake wire can also be used. Alternatively 28 gauge uncovered wire may be used. (A heavier uncovered wire must be used.)

Ironing cloth fine cotton - placed between iron and satin when ironing on bonding web - so you don't scorch the satin and the tracing lines don't smudge. It also stops your iron from picking up any of the bonding 'glue'!

HANDY HINT
To ensure longevity of your embroidery you may prefer to use acid free cardboard and acid free glue.

BEFORE YOU BEGIN

Take the creamy gold satin which is the main background fabric and cut out 24 pieces of fabric 15 cm square (6") to fit into a 10 cm (4") embroidery hoop.

Cut 24 pieces of backing fabric approximately 15cms (6") square - this is used behind all embroidery.

Gather together the additional materials required and prepare the pieces for each decoration before you begin the stitching (the fun part) and you will achieve the results much more quickly than if you have to stop to find things, cut up fabric shapes and so on. Refer to the detailed instructions given with each decoration you plan to stitch for the design to trace, satin and threads to use and any other materials required.

Backing fabric is *always* used behind the satin for all the embroidery in this book.

Refer to each design for detailed instructions on the order of working each decoration.

EGLANTINE ROSE

The Eglantine Rose was a symbol of purity and adopted by Elizabeth as her personal emblem. Elizabeth I shared her fellow countrymen's joy in flowers and house gardens - a new addition to the English way of life. They had previously been confined to great monastic foundations and walled castles but in this period they became general for large homes also. Flowers were embroidered on gowns, jackets, cushions and furnishing. Elizabeth was painted with them tucked in her hair and in some portraits she is shown holding a flower.

Refer to colour photograph on page 38

THREADS

Colour	DMC	Anchor	Au Ver a Soie -D'Alger	Madeira
White	Blanc	White	Blanc	White
Dark Green	30895*	246	1836	1514

*rayon one thread used, stranded cotton or silk use two threads

REQUIREMENTS
- Fine gold metallic thread DMC 282
- Beads Gold Metallic Seed
- 30 gauge white covered wire
- contact, tracing paper and calico

DESIGN TO TRACE

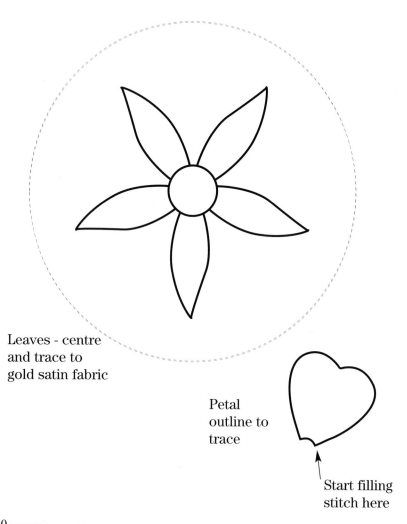

Leaves - centre
and trace to
gold satin fabric

Petal
outline to
trace

Start filling
stitch here

This rose is made with needle lace. The petals are created individually and then sewn to the fabric to create a multi-petalled, three-dimensional, flower.

TO EMBROIDER THE DESIGN

Centre the leaves and trace on to the gold satin fabric. Put the gold satin with backing into a frame and embroider the leaves in fishbone stitch using one thread of dark green rayon. Although only a small section of each leaf is seen between the petals, they are stitched up to the central circle of the rose - see design to trace. This ensures that the needle lace petals are slightly raised.

The central area is left unstitched and the needle lace petals are attached here before sewing the gold beads on the surface.

Couch round each leaf with fine gold metallic thread. See page 14 for more information on couching.

The five white needle lace petals are each worked individually in punto in aria or needle lace. Trace outline given five times and work following the instructions for punto in aria petals given on page 18. Use fine wire as the 'foundation thread' and doubled white sewing cotton as the couching thread.

You will find the wire is very pliable and bends easily. When overlapping the wire keep the ends tight and close together to prevent 'bulk'.

Start working detached buttonhole stitch at the base of each petal using two threads of white stranded cotton. I used detached buttonhole stitch to make the petals firmer. Fill area. (Refer to page 20 for more information on working detached buttonhole stitch.) To complete, work buttonhole stitches very closely together all round the edge with fine metallic gold thread.

Remove the completed needle lace petals from the calico by cutting the couching threads between the two layers of calico and then stitch the petals in position, leaving about 1cm (1/2") in diameter in the centre to fill with gold seed beads. When the decoration is assembled (see page 76) gently fold petals forward to form a "cup".

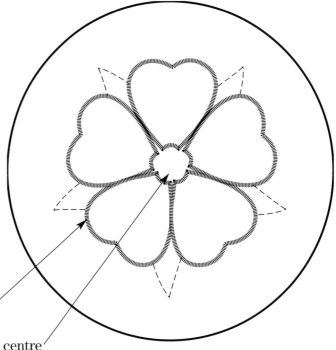

Buttonhole stitch worked using fine gold metallic thread

Sew gold seed beads in centre

– – – – – – – fine gold metallic thread

THE BUTTERFLY

Refer to colour photograph on page 38

The Elizabethan embroiderers' love of flowers and the small animals and insects that lived in and near them is shown in their embroidery. They embroidered animals and birds and an amazing array of worms, caterpillars, spiders, butterflies and unidentifiable insects to fill all available space. Their sizing and colouring frequently bear little resemblance to the real thing but were still most attractive in their embroidery as they are in modern embroidery.

THREADS

Colour	DMC	Anchor	Au Ver a Soie -D'Alger	Madeira
Dark Brown	938	380	4132	2005
Sunset Red	350	11	913	0213
Sunset Orange	3825	1047	643	0307
Sunset Pink	352	9	922	0303

REQUIREMENTS
- Fine gold metallic thread DMC 282
- Beads: 6 coral coloured seed beads, 6 brown coloured seed beads
- 30 gauge white covered wire
- contact, tracing paper and calico

DESIGN TO TRACE

TO EMBROIDER THE DESIGN

Trace the outline of the butterfly, see design to trace and
work following the instructions for punto in aria given on
page 18.

Use the white covered fine wire as the 'foundation thread'.
Bend it to the shape of the butterfly, overlapping the wire *at
the centre base of the wing.* You will find the wire is very
pliable and bends easily. When overlapping the wire keep the
ends tight and close together to prevent 'bulk'.
Use doubled cream sewing cotton as the couching thread.

The wings are worked in one piece. Start working single
Brussels stitch at the left hand edge of the wing where
indicated, using two threads of dark brown stranded cotton.
(Refer to page 23 for more information on working single
Brussels stitch.) Referring to the diagram shade the wing
from dark brown, to sunset red, sunset orange and sunset
pink. To create the 'wavy' lines of the butterflies wings adjust
the tension of the stitches by pulling the thread tighter when
working the first row with a new colour, see fig. 2.

When you reach the centre, stop and run the thread through
the stitches covering the wire to finish. Then go to the outer
edge of the second wing and work into the centre repeating
the shading. Work the last row of the second side into the

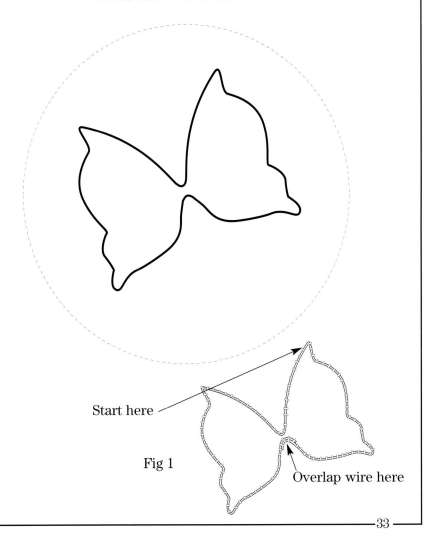

Start here

Fig 1

Overlap wire here

last row of stitching on the first side so that the wings are one piece. Work buttonhole stitches very closely together round the edge of the wings with fine metallic gold thread. If your stitching looks a little 'sparse' work another row over the top! To complete, attach beads where indicated. Remove the needle lace wings from the calico by cutting the couching threads between the two layers of calico, they are now ready to attach to the gold satin.

If required trace the outline of the body onto the centre of the gold satin before it is put in the hoop to embroider. (Remember the needle lace wings will be placed over the top of part of the tracing.) Place the gold satin fabric with backing in the hoop then stitch the wings in the centre of the gold satin fabric.

Embroider the body, head and antennae over the top of the centre of the needle lace wings in satin stitch using one thread of dark brown. To outline the body, couch fine gold thread around it. When you have joined the front and back of the decoration together (see page 76) bend the wings forward and it looks as if the butterfly has just alighted for a short time on the fabric!

HANDY HINT
Use old snips or scissors to cut the wire

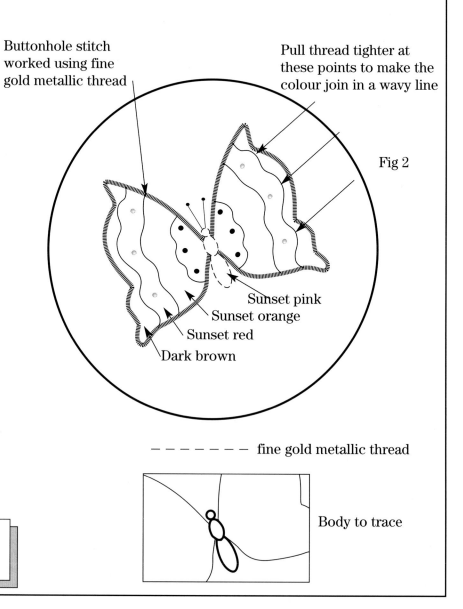

Buttonhole stitch worked using fine gold metallic thread

Pull thread tighter at these points to make the colour join in a wavy line

Fig 2

Sunset pink
Sunset orange
Sunset red
Dark brown

— — — — — — fine gold metallic thread

Body to trace

THE KNIGHT

A suit of armour was frequently worn by gentlemen when taking part in festive tilts held to honour Queen Elizabeth's Accession Day. These light hearted occasions were celebrated across the country. The suit of armour was made up of many pieces which fitted together to form the suit.

Refer to colour photograph on page 37

REQUIREMENTS
- Fine gold metallic thread DMC 282
- Craft metallic gold (1mm)
- Gold coloured sewing thread for couching on the metallic threads
- Small piece of royal blue satin
- Bead: 1 x 1 mm gold metallic

Trace the outline and couching lines of the knight onto the blue satin (see design to trace). Next cut out a square of bonding web bigger than the knight and iron the bonding web onto *the back* of the blue satin. Cut carefully round the design, peel off the paper, place the knight in the centre of the gold satin square right side up and iron in place. Always place an ironing cloth between the blue satin and the iron to protect the satin.

Put the gold satin fabric with backing into a frame then couch the craft metallic gold round the outline of the knight, his jacket, the helmet and the edge of the gauntlets.

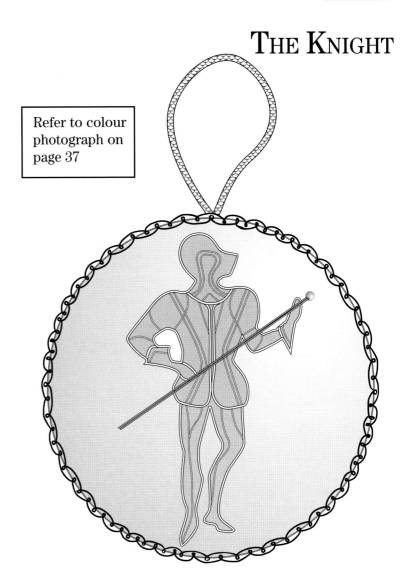

The staff is two strands of craft metallic gold laid side by side and couched as one. When couching designs like these with lots of small lines and only small distances between them, just carry the thread at the back of the work rather than cutting and re-starting. On the diagram the craft metallic gold is shown with a solid line and the armour details, couched with fine gold metallic thread are shown with a dotted line. Stitch the bead on to the end of the staff. Make up the decoration as described on page 76.

DESIGN TO TRACE

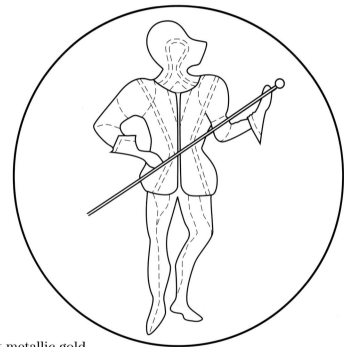

——————— craft metallic gold

– – – – – – – fine gold metallic thread

○ beads

THE FALCON

THE KNIGHT

EGLANTINE ROSE

THE BUTTERFLY

THE BOOT

'UNDRESS' CAP

THE LUTE

40

ALTERNATIVELY
THESE
DECORATIONS
WOULD LOOK
ATTRACTIVE
DISPLAYED
ON THE
MANTEL
OR WALL

THE GLOVE

'SWETE' BAG

42

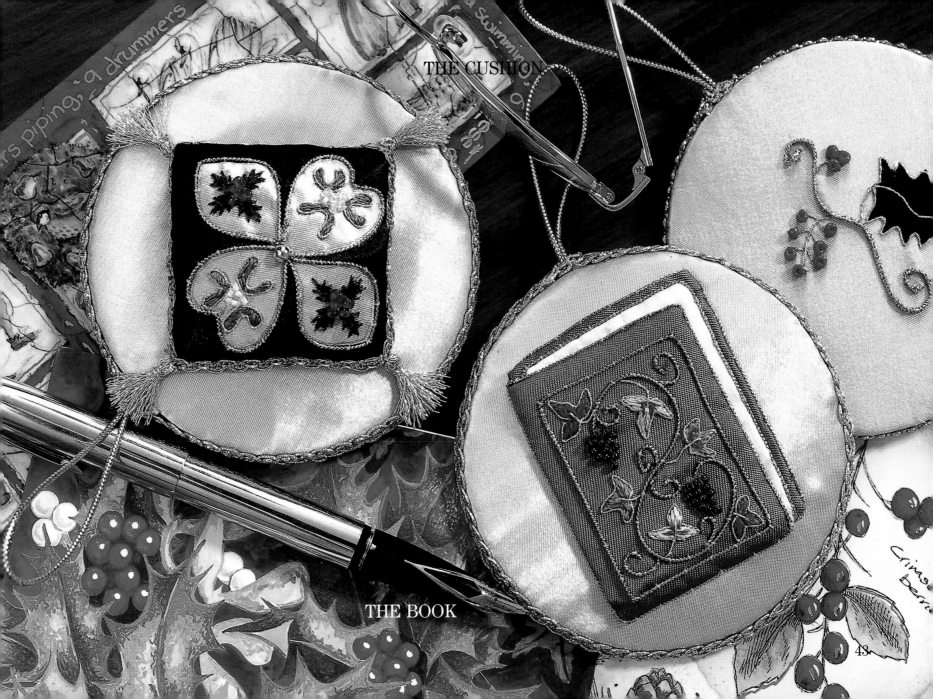

THE CUSHION

THE BOOK

THE BOOT

Elizabeth I had literally hundreds of pairs of different types of footwear, from slip on shoes to boots for riding. Some were lined with velvet or satin. Boots such as these were used for riding and known as 'buskins'. Men also wore highly decorated boots.

Refer to colour photograph on page 39

REQUIREMENTS

- Fine gold metallic thread DMC 282
- Craft metallic gold (1mm)
- Gold coloured sewing thread for couching on the metallic threads and sewing on beads
- Small piece of Maroon Satin
- Beads - 17 Peacock coloured seed beads

Trace the outline and couching lines of the boot onto the maroon satin (see design to trace). Next cut out a square of bonding web bigger than the boot and iron the bonding web onto *the back* of the maroon satin. Cut carefully round the design, peel off the paper, place the boot in the centre of the gold satin square right side up and iron in place. Always place an ironing cloth between the satin and the iron to protect the satin.

Put the gold satin fabric with backing into a frame then couch the craft metallic gold round the outline of the boot including the side seam and the seam up the instep.

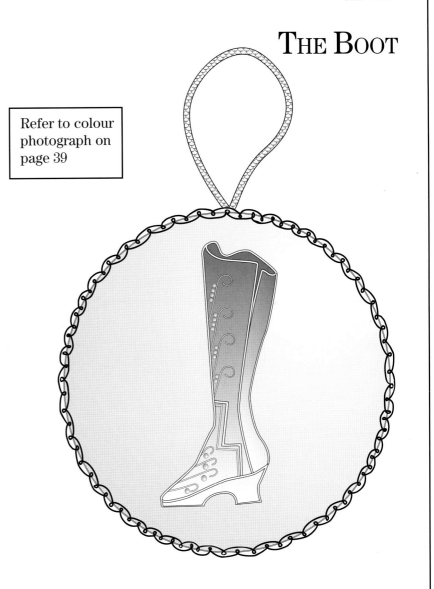

On the diagram the craft metallic gold is shown with a solid line and the details, side seam and the seam up the instep, couched with fine gold metallic thread are shown with a dotted line. When couching designs like these with lots of small lines and only small distances between them, just carry the thread at the back of the work rather than cutting and re-

starting. To complete the boot peacock coloured seed beads are sewn where indicated.

Assemble the 'boot' decoration following the instructions given on page 76.

DESIGN TO TRACE

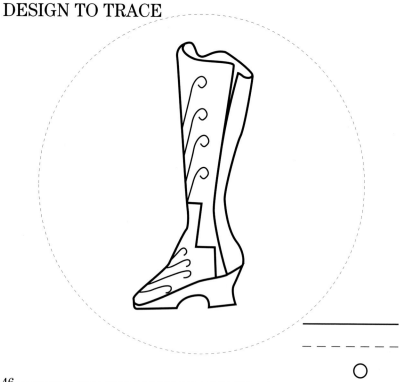

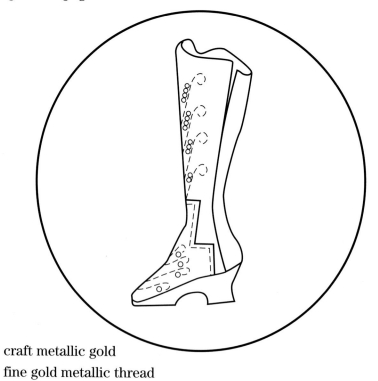

—————————— craft metallic gold

– – – – – – – – fine gold metallic thread

○ beads

THE GLOVE

Gloves were a fashionable accessory worn, or more often carried, by both men and women of the period. They were a conspicuous mark of rank, an essential item of finery and made of doeskin and embroidered they were an expensive, but very acceptable gift. Later in the period the gloves were cut to have seams from the fingers that extended well onto the back of the hand, giving the impression of very long fingers! The embroidery on the cuff was worked using coloured silk threads and silver, or gold gilt stitched on silk or satin this was then attached to the leather.

Refer to colour photograph on page 42

REQUIREMENTS

• Fine gold metallic thread DMC 282
• Craft metallic gold (1mm)
• Gold coloured sewing thread for couching on the metallic threads and sewing on beads
• Small piece of Crushed Strawberry satin
• Approx. 35 variegated mauve seed beads

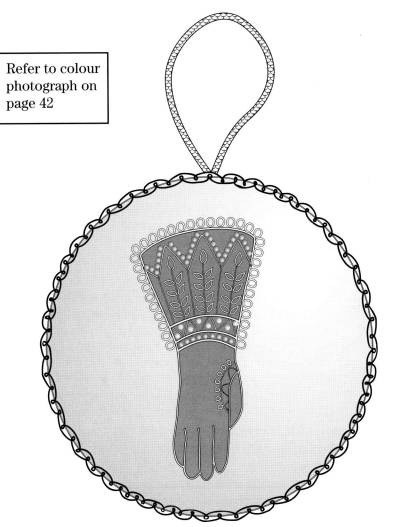

Trace the outline and couching lines of the glove onto the strawberry satin (see design to trace). Next cut out a square of bonding web bigger than the glove and iron the bonding web onto the back of the strawberry satin. Cut carefully round the design, peel off the paper, place the glove in the centre of the gold satin square right side up and iron in place. Always place an ironing cloth between the satin and the iron to protect the satin.

DESIGN TO TRACE

HANDY HINT
Keep needle threaded with fine metallic gold thread
so that you can carry thread to new position
without having to stop and start thread

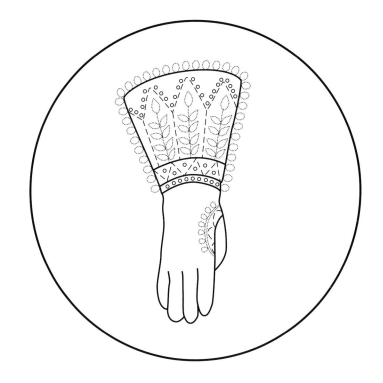

——————————— craft metallic gold

– – – – – – – fine gold metallic thread

◯ beads

Put the gold satin fabric with backing into a frame then couch the craft metallic gold round the outline of the glove including the thumb and across the wrist. On the diagram the craft metallic gold is shown with a solid line and the details including the zig zag at the upper and lower edges of the cuff, couched with fine gold metallic thread are shown with a dotted line. When couching designs like these with lots of small lines and only small distances between them, just carry the thread at the back of the work rather than cutting and re-starting.

The cuff is decorated with a leaf pattern worked in single chain stitches using fine gold metallic thread. Couch the fine gold metallic thread down the centre of the design, then work single chain stitches to create the leaf pattern. Using the same thread work single Brussels stitch around the cuff edge to create the effect of a lace edging round the gloves. This is also worked by the thumb - see diagram. To complete attach the beads to the glove following the diagram.

Assemble the 'glove' decoration following the instructions given on page 76.

THE FALCON

Refer to colour photograph on page 37

Falcons were popular in Elizabethan society. Hunting was the pastime of the rich as owning and maintaining the birds was expensive. The hawking hoods and gloves were richly embroidered usually in velvet with embossed leather. The frequently wayward behaviour of hawks (they were known to vanish into the blue after large expense and long hours of sometimes frustrating devotion) meant that they were identified with jesses and bells so any countryman coming across them would know they belonged to the local aristocrat and their return would be rewarded!

THREADS

Colour	DMC	Anchor	Au Ver a Soie -D'Alger	Madeira
Turquoise	30995*	410	115	1102
Golden yellow	30676*	891	2532	2208

*rayon one thread used, stranded cotton or silk use two threads

REQUIREMENTS

- Fine gold metallic thread DMC 282
- Craft metallic gold (1mm)
- Gold coloured sewing thread for couching on the metallic threads

No. 1 DESIGN TO TRACE
to turquoise satin

No. 2 DESIGN TO TRACE
to gold satin (includes beak head etc.)

- Small piece of turquoise satin
- Beads: 1 x 1 mm Gold Metallic Bead, 3 x Gold Metallic Seed Beads, 1 x 1mm red glass bead, 2 x white purled seed beads

Trace the outline and couching lines of the falcon onto the turquoise satin (see No. 1 design to trace). Note - when tracing the outline of the falcon to the turquoise satin do not trace the beak, head feathers, crown and legs. Next cut out a square of bonding web bigger than the falcon and iron the

bonding web onto the back of the turquoise satin. Cut carefully round the design, peel off the paper, place the falcon in the centre of the gold satin square right side up and iron in place. Always place an ironing cloth between the turquoise satin and the iron to protect the satin.

Once the falcon's body is ironed securely to the main gold satin fabric, trace the head feathers, crown, beak and legs on to the satin (from No. 2 design to trace).

Put the gold satin fabric with backing into a frame then embroider the head feathers in satin stitch using turquoise. The legs, feet, beak and crown are worked in satin stitch using golden yellow.

On the diagram the craft metallic gold is shown with a solid line. It is couched around the edge of the turquoise satin and down the edge of the falcon's chest on the right. The details, couched with fine gold metallic thread are shown with a dotted line. This is couched around the beak, head feathers, crown, legs and feet.

Still using fine gold metallic thread work the body feathers on the falcon's chest and top of his wings in fly stitches and the long feathers on the wings and tail in straight stitches.

Attach a 1 mm gold bead for the falcon's eye and three gold seed beads, one on each tip of the crown. At the base of the crown sew one red bead in the centre with a pearl seed bead on either side to complete.

Assemble the 'falcon' decoration following the instructions given on page 76.

—————————— craft metallic gold

- - - - - - - - fine gold metallic thread

◯ beads

THE LION AND UNICORN

The Lion and the Unicorn are the Royal Coat of Arms, they are on the Great Seal, and a modern Lion and Unicorn are the central figures on The Queen Mother's Gate installed in 1993 at the South East entrance to Hyde Park in London. The lion is the emblem of England and the horn from the Unicorn was said, in Elizabethan times, to be a protection from poisons when used as a vessel (in fact the horns of rhinoceros were used). The Lion and Unicorn also feature one on each pillar guarding the gates at Hampton Court Palace.

Refer to colour photograph on page 41

REQUIREMENTS

- Fine gold metallic thread DMC 282
- Craft metallic gold (1mm)
- Gold coloured sewing thread for couching on the metallic threads and beads
- Small pieces of light brown satin for the Lion, gold for the
- Crown and White for the Unicorn
- Beads: 1 x 2 mm gold metallic, 2 x 1 mm gold metallic, 2 x gold metallic seed beads, 8 x white purled seed beads, 4 x red glass seed beads

Trace the outlines and couching lines of the Lion on to the brown satin, the Crown on the gold satin and the Unicorn on the white satin (see design to trace). Next cut out squares of bonding web bigger than the Lion, Crown and Unicorn and iron the bonding web onto *the back* of each of the three pieces of satin. Cut carefully round the designs, peel off the paper, place the three shapes in the correct positions in the centre of the gold satin circle right side up and iron in place. Always place an ironing cloth between the satin and the iron so that the satin is not scorched.

To ensure correct positioning of the Lion, Unicorn and Crown trace the design onto paper with a heavy black outline that can be seen through the satin. Lay the main fabric over the design, checking the design is in the centre. Lay the cut out shape of the Lion over the lion (traced below) iron on. Then lay the cut out shape of the Unicorn over the tracing of the Unicorn, iron on. Do the same for the crown. This will ensure they are all positioned correctly.

DESIGN TO TRACE

——————————— craft metallic gold

– – – – – – – fine gold metallic thread

O beads

Place the gold satin fabric with backing, into a frame then couch the craft metallic gold round the outlines of each of the three shapes plus the base of the lion's mane and the inside line of the crown. The unicorn mane and tail, the lion's mane and crown decoration are couched with fine gold metallic thread.

On the diagram the craft metallic gold is shown with a solid line, the details, couched with fine gold metallic thread, are shown with a dotted line.

Sew the two gold seed beads on as eyes, one each for the Lion and Unicorn. The 1 mm and 2 mm gold beads are sewn on the crown, the 2 mm bead at the centre, the 1 mm on either side. The red and white beads are sewn at the base of the crown see photograph page 41.

Assemble the decoration following the instructions given on page 76.

THE LUTE

Refer to colour photograph on page 40

The printing press helped the advancement of English music and also enabled it to be enjoyed by many. Elizabeth I was considered to be an accomplished musician and liked to play the lute in her Privy Chambers with her closest courtiers. Elizabeth I enjoyed music and dancing well into her old age.

REQUIREMENTS

- Black stranded cotton or silk
- Fine gold metallic thread DMC 282
- Craft metallic gold (1mm)
- Gold coloured sewing thread for couching on the metallic threads
- Small piece of white satin
- Small piece of brown satin or gold flecked brown fabric
- Small piece of heavy duty vilene
- 1 gold bugle bead
- Fine cardboard for the lute

Trace the outline of the sheet of music plus the notes and music lines onto the white satin (see design to trace). Next cut out a square of bonding web bigger than the sheet of music and iron the bonding web onto *the back* of the white satin. Cut carefully round the design, peel off the paper, place the sheet of music in the centre of the gold satin square right side up and iron in place. Always place an ironing cloth between the white satin and the iron so that the satin is not scorched.

DESIGNS TO TRACE

Put the gold satin fabric with backing into a frame then using one thread of black stranded work the lines for the music in long straight stitches and the notes in short straight stitches. The notes are actually diamond shaped as this is how they were drawn at the time. Couch round the 'sheet of music' with craft metallic gold.

The Lute is three dimensional. This is achieved very cleverly and quite simply! Trace the shape of the Lute onto the heavy duty vilene cut this out and then draw round this onto the piece of fine cardboard and cut out. Stick the vilene shape on to cardboard with double sided tape. With the cardboard template as your pattern, trace the Lute shape on to the right side of the brown fabric but do not cut out at this stage.

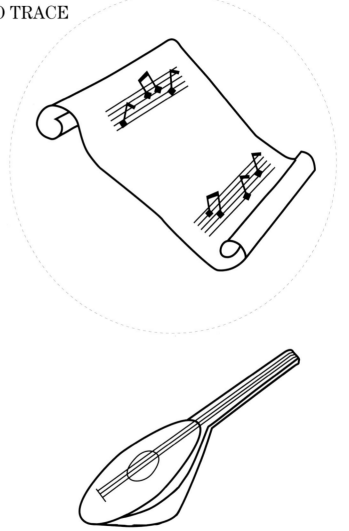

HANDY HINT
If you use heavier fabric than satin for the lute it may not need to be backed.

Place the brown satin with backing into a frame and couch craft metallic gold round the main outlines, refer to the diagram where the placement of craft metallic gold is shown with solid lines. With one thread of black stranded cotton, work the hole in the centre of the lute in satin stitch.

Attach the bugle bead where shown on diagram. Couch fine gold metallic thread round the hole and add the strings with long straight stitches. These are couched at the upper end only. The placement of this thread is shown with dotted lines.

Now take the brown fabric out of the frame and cut the lute shape out leaving a 1cm (1/2") seam allowance all round. Trim the backing right back to the exact shape of the lute. When lacing the fabric over the lute shape start at the 'neck' of the lute. The fabric here will have to be trimmed back even further before it is laced. Turn the top end in first then turn the two sides in over it before lacing the two edges together firmly, work down the shape of the lute.

When the lacing is completed place the lute in the correct position on the gold satin background fabric, positioning the lute between the music, sew in place.

Assemble the 'Lute' decoration following the instructions given on page 76.

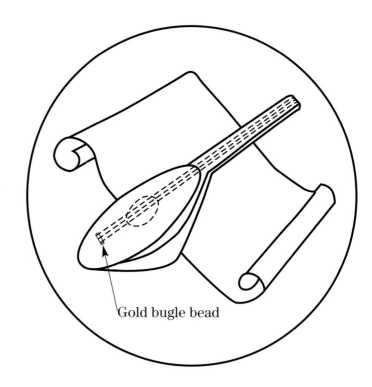

Gold bugle bead

———————— craft metallic gold

– – – – – – – fine gold metallic thread

THE CUSHION

Refer to colour photograph on page 43

Cushions were ornately embroidered by Elizabethan's for use in their homes. They were used to soften the hard forms they sat upon and varied in size from square to a long and narrow rectangle. They also stitched cushions to rest books, particularly the Bible, on. The books in themselves were precious and if the book had a richly embroidered cover encrusted with jewels this would need to be separated from any hard surface. The backs of cushions were never embroidered. Pincushions, small and rectangular, were also richly worked in raised embroidery. These were essential items of everyday living, as all costumes were either pinned or laced together.

THREADS

Colour	DMC	Anchor	Au Ver a Soie -D'Alger	Madeira
Dark green	30895*	246	1846	1514
Mid green	30702*	226	224	1306

*rayon one thread used, stranded cotton or silk use two threads

REQUIREMENTS

- Fine gold metallic thread DMC 282
- Craft metallic gold
- Stranded Metallic Gold DMC
- Gold coloured sewing thread for couching on the metallic threads
- Green sewing cotton to match cushion
- 25 cm (10") length of 3 mm (3/16") wide metallic gold braid
- Small pieces of dark green and cream satin
- Small piece of heavy duty vilene
- Dacron stuffing, small quantity
- Beads: 8 x red glass seed, 10 x white purled seed, 1 x 2 mm metallic gold bead

The cushion is raised and padded making it three dimensional and very charming.
It is worked in stages. First trace the outline of the central design and the leaf shapes that are embroidered on it, on to the cream satin. Next cut out a square of bonding web bigger than the central design and iron the bonding web onto the back of the cream satin. Cut carefully round the design, peel off the paper, place the cream satin in the centre of the dark green satin square right side up and iron in place. Place an ironing cloth between the satin and the iron so that the satin is not scorched and the pencil or carbon lines do not smudge.

DESIGN TO TRACE

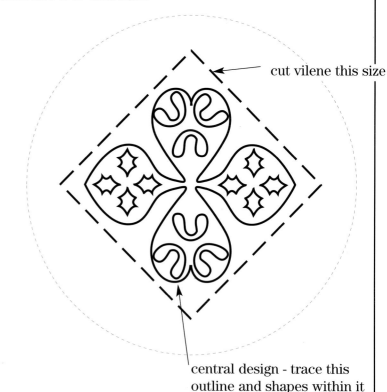

cut vilene this size

central design - trace this outline and shapes within it onto cream satin

Place the green satin and backing, with the cream satin already appliqued to it into the hoop to work.

The holly is worked in fishbone stitch using one thread of dark green. The mistletoe leaves are worked in satin stitch using one thread of mid green.

Couch craft metallic gold round the cream appliqued design shape and fine gold metallic thread round the mistletoe leaves. On the diagram the craft metallic gold is shown with a solid line and the fine gold metallic thread is shown with a dotted line.

Sew the 2 mm gold bead at the centre of the cushion and then sew four red beads for berries in the centre of the holly leaves and five white beads in the centre of the mistletoe leaves.

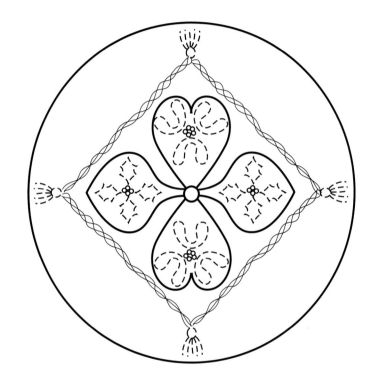

———————— craft metallic gold

— — — — — — fine gold metallic thread

○ beads

Remove the 'cushion top' from your embroidery hoop. Cut a piece of heavy duty vilene the exact size of the cushion, trim off surplus backing and green satin, leaving about 3 cm to fold back over the vilene neatly. I leave 3 cm (1") as this adds to the 'stuffing' effect. Lace the 'cushion' firmly round the vilene keeping the corners neat.

Place a piece of the gold satin background fabric, with backing, in your embroidery hoop. Centre the cushion on the background fabric and pin each corner in place then slip stitch along three sides. Stuff a little Dacron evenly in the open side. Stitch down final side, then stitch 3 mm (3/16") gold braid round the edge of the cushion.

Make four little tassels by wrapping the gold stranded metallic thread round a 16 mm (3/4") wide strip of card about four times. Thread a length of fine gold metallic thread in your needle, slip the needle through all the wraps at one end of the card and slide the tassel off. Wrap thread around the tassel near the top a few times, fasten off securely. Trim the ends and stitch one tassel on at each corner.

Assemble the 'cushion' decoration following the instructions given on page 76.

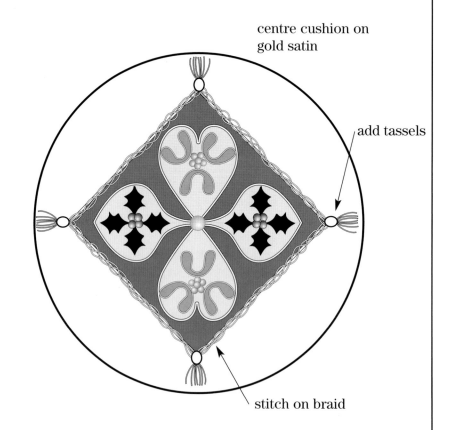

centre cushion on gold satin

add tassels

stitch on braid

'SWETE' BAG

Elizabethan women did not have pockets in any of their clothes and there are many sixteenth century bags, sometimes with matching pincushions, in good repair extant so it is possible they were not used a lot. They were made of silk, satin or canvas work, using a variety of stitches. A feature of these bags is the trimmings. They had a drawstring top with multi-coloured cords. In addition they had ornamental tassels and fringes. It is thought they were used to hold a seal, charm, counters, dice, perfume or pot pourri. They may have held a New Year's gift of money or jewellery.

Refer to colour photograph on page 42

THREADS

Colour	DMC	Anchor	Au Ver a Soie -D'Alger	Madeira
Dark pink-tulip	33607 *	87	1042	0708
Light pink - carnation	33689*	49	3031	0607
Blue - rose	30932*	343	1713	1710
Mauve - Pansy	30554*	96	1312	0711
Dark mauve - Pansy	30552*	99	1314	0712

*rayon one thread used, stranded cotton or silk use two threads

REQUIREMENTS

- Fine gold metallic thread DMC 282
- Craft metallic gold (1mm)
- Crinkle metallic gold
- Stranded metallic gold DMC
- Gold coloured sewing thread for couching on the metallic threads
- Blue coloured sewing cotton to match bag
- Small piece of mid Blue Satin
- Small piece of heavy duty Vilene
- Beads: 3 x 1 mm gold metallic, 1 small bugle blue green, 1 dark blue seed

The 'Swete bag' is embroidered separately and then applied to the background satin. It is worked in stages. First trace the *design only* on to the blue satin, (*do not trace* the outline of the bag - the long dashed line - as the edge, when folded over the vilene may not be exactly where the outline was drawn). Place the satin and backing fabric in the hoop ready to embroider the different flowers.

Embroider the tulip in satin stitch using one thread of dark pink. The carnation is worked in straight stitches using one thread of light pink. The rose is embroidered with long bullions using one thread of blue. Refer to page 16 for full

DESIGN TO TRACE

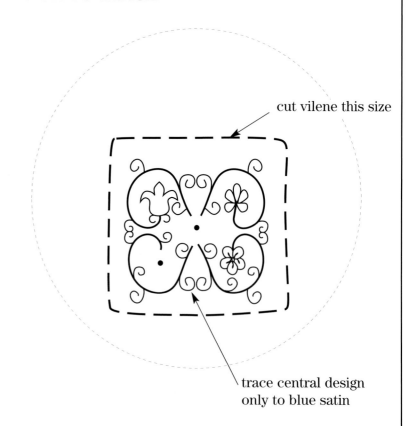

cut vilene this size

trace central design
only to blue satin

instructions on working long bullion stitch. Alternatively this may be worked in satin stitch.

The pansy is worked in satin stitch using one thread of mauve with a straight stitch in dark mauve at the centre of each petal. The centre daisy is worked in detached chain using fine gold metallic thread.

Couch the thicker scrolls with craft metallic gold and the finer 'curls' with fine gold metallic thread, couch this round the edges of the petals of the tulip and pansy also.
On the diagram the craft metallic gold is shown with a solid line and the fine gold metallic thread is shown with a dotted line.

To complete your 'swete bag' sew a gold bead at the centre of the daisy and the pansy and one at the base of the tulip. Sew a blue bead at the centre of the rose and the small bugle at the base of the carnation.

Remove the embroidered 'swete bag' from your hoop. Cut a piece of heavy duty vilene to the exact shape of the bag, trim off surplus backing and blue satin fabric, leaving about 2 cm (3/4") to fold back over the vilene neatly. Lace the 'swete' bag firmly round the vilene keeping the corners neat.

————————	craft metallic gold
– – – – – – –	fine gold metallic thread
··················	crinkle metallic gold
◯	beads

Place a piece of the gold satin background fabric with backing in your hoop and slip stitch the 'swete bag' on to the main fabric in the correct position leaving the top edge open.

Thread crinkle metallic gold across the top edge of the bag as shown, leaving a small length each end which is used to loop through the tassel. Couch crinkle metallic gold in place to form the handle as shown in the diagram.

Make five little tassels by wrapping the gold stranded metallic thread round a 16 mm (3/4") wide strip of card about four times. Thread a length of fine metallic gold thread in your needle, slip the needle through all the wraps at one end of the card and slide the tassel off. Wrap thread around the tassel near the top a few times, fasten off securely.

Thread the two ends at the top of the bag through the middle of the tassel tops before taking the ends to the back of the embroidery and finishing.

To make the loops at the base of the bag, bring the needle, threaded with crinkle metallic gold, to the front near the corner, (see diagram) take the needle through the centre of the tassel then through the fabric to the back and finish off. Repeat at the centre and the far side.

Assemble the 'cushion' decoration following the instructions given on page 76.

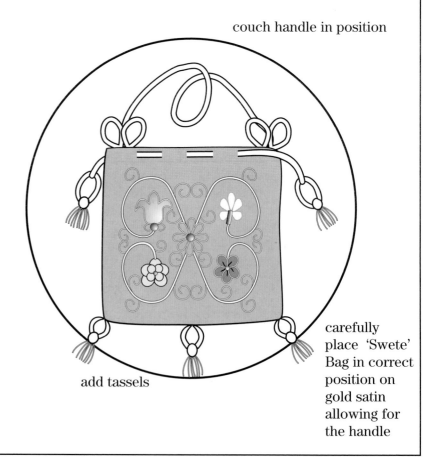

couch handle in position

carefully place 'Swete' Bag in correct position on gold satin allowing for the handle

add tassels

'UNDRESS' CAP

Refer to colour photograph on page 39

When women wore a coif, men wore an 'undress' or 'night' cap. They were worn indoors but were not worn to bed - a 'biggin' cap was worn then. They were usually embroidered on linen using coloured silks and gold or silver but there are examples worked in blackwork and whitework.

REQUIREMENTS
- DMC Rayon Green 30911, Anchor 230, Madeira 1301, Au Ver a Soie D'Alger 213
- Fine gold metallic thread DMC 282
- Craft metallic gold
- Gold coloured sewing thread for couching on the metallic threads
- Red sewing cotton to match cap
- Small piece of red satin
- Small piece of heavy duty Vilene
- Beads: white purled seed

DESIGN TO TRACE

The 'Undress Cap' is embroidered separately and then applied to the background satin. It is worked in stages. First trace the design on to the red satin, (see design to trace, but *do not* trace the outline of the cap - the long dashed line - as the edge, when folded over the vilene may not be exactly where the outline was drawn). Place the red satin and backing fabric in the hoop ready to embroider. All the leaves are worked in fishbone stitch using one thread of green.

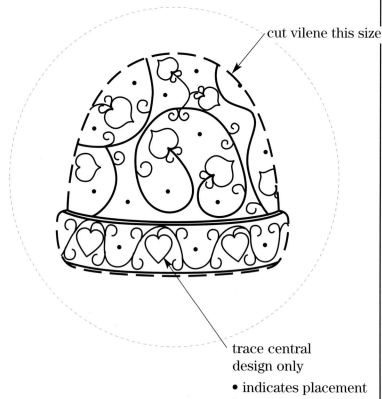

cut vilene this size

trace central design only

• indicates placement for groups of beads

Next couch the craft metallic gold in place. The fine tendrils are added last. These are couched using fine gold metallic thread. On the diagram the craft metallic gold is shown with a solid line and the fine gold metallic thread is shown with a dotted line. Couch the scrolls individually (beginning one end finishing the other).

The flowers are clusters of five white purled seed beads which are attached last filling in the gaps!

Trace the outline of the cap onto heavy duty vilene and cut out. Remove the embroidered cap from your hoop and trim off surplus backing and excess satin fabric, leaving about 2 cm (3/4") to fold back over the vilene cap shape neatly. Lace the cap firmly over the vilene.

Place the gold satin background fabric and backing in your hoop and slip stitch the cap on to the main fabric in the correct position leaving the lower edge open.

Assemble the decoration following the instructions given on page 76.

———————— craft metallic gold

– – – – – – fine gold metallic thread

◯ beads

Book Cover

Refer to colour photograph on page 43

Books were treasured possessions. Their bindings were usually of velvet and canvas work although some later ones were made of silk, this was not such a practical material. A book would be kept in a drawstring bag for protection, and a cushion would be placed underneath when in use. A number of richly embroidered Book Covers from Elizabethan times still exist, including a book cover embroidered by Elizabeth as an 11 year old, for her stepmother Katherine Parr, then Queen. This example is worked on blue cloth with an intricate knot work pattern embroidered in silver thread.

Threads

Colour	DMC	Anchor	Au Ver a Soie -D'Alger	Madeira
Golden yellow	30676*	891	2532	2208
Autumn red	30498*	1006	2925	0511
Rust brown	30976*	308	2546	2302

*rayon one thread used, stranded cotton or silk use two threads

REQUIREMENTS

- Fine gold metallic thread DMC 282
- Craft metallic gold (1mm)
- Gold coloured sewing cotton for couching on the metallic threads
- Small pieces of green and white satin, allow for turnings
- Small piece of heavy duty Vilene
- Beads - Mill Hill Garnet 00367 Seed

The Book is made using similar techniques to those used in making the 'Swete Bag' and 'Undress' Cap. It is made up of three layers, each layer is made separately then the three layers are assembled making the 'book'.

First trace the front cover design on to the green satin, but *do not* trace the outline of the book - long dashed line - as the edge, when folded over the vilene may not be exactly where the outline was drawn. Place the green satin and backing fabric in the hoop ready to embroider. All the leaves are worked in fishbone stitch using one thread of red in the two corner leaves, one thread of rust brown in the two central leaves and one thread of golden yellow in the remaining two leaves. Work three or four little straight stitches in the centre of the golden yellow and rust brown leaves using one thread of autumn red to accentuate the autumn tones.

DESIGN TO TRACE
front cover

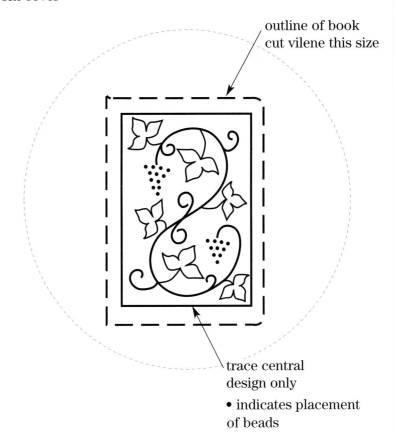

outline of book
cut vilene this size

trace central
design only

• indicates placement
of beads

Next couch the craft metallic gold round the square just outside the central design and on the main scroll shape. The stems of the leaves are worked using fine gold metallic thread. Still using this thread couch round the outer edge of all the leaves. On the diagram the craft metallic gold is shown with a solid line and fine gold metallic thread is shown with a dotted line.

Sew garnet coloured beads in position to make clumps of grapes.

Cut two pieces of vilene, one the size of the back cover and the other the size of the front cover see designs to be traced.

Remove the embroidered book cover from your hoop, trim off surplus backing and excess satin fabric, leaving about 2 cm (3/4") all round. Take the piece of vilene for the front cover and fold the embroidery over it, tucking raw edges to the back and keeping the corners neat. Lace the embroidery firmly over the vilene. Put to one side.

Cut a piece of green satin for the back cover big enough to cover the 'vilene back cover' plus a 1 cm (1/2") seam allowance on all sides. Cut a piece of white satin the same size. Fold the green satin over the vilene back cover tucking the raw edges to the back of the vilene and lace edges together firmly, keeping the corners neat.

DESIGN TO TRACE
back cover

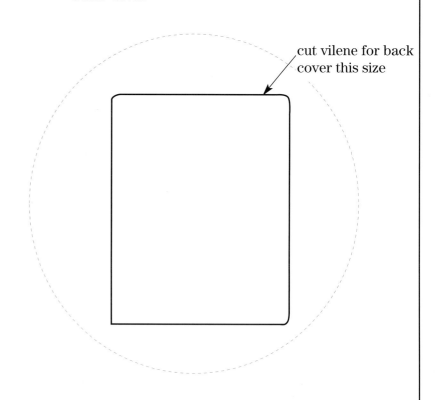

cut vilene for back cover this size

Place the gold satin background fabric and backing in your hoop and slip stitch the back cover on to the main fabric in the correct position. Now turn under the top and right hand edge of the white satin and slip stitch onto the green satin back cover. The other two edges are left raw as they are covered by the front cover.

Finally place the front cover in position, trim back the white satin 'pages' so that they do not show beyond the left hand or lower edge of the front cover and slip stitch the front cover in place. Couch Craft metallic gold around the edges of the front and back covers and the white 'pages', refer to the diagram for its placement.

Assemble the decoration following the instructions given on page 76.

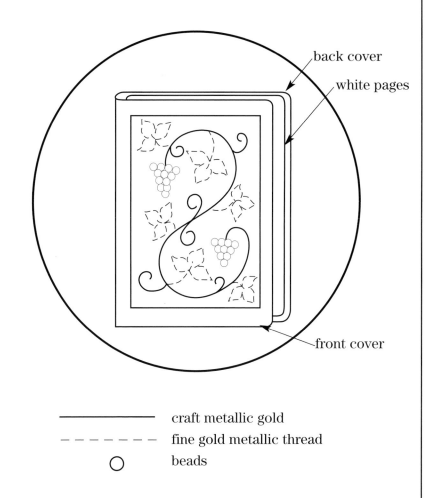

back cover

white pages

front cover

———————— craft metallic gold

– – – – – – – fine gold metallic thread

○ beads

HOLLY LEAVES AND BERRIES
- THE BACK OF EACH DESIGN

Refer to colour photograph on page 43

REQUIREMENTS

- Fine gold metallic thread DMC 282
- Craft metallic gold (1mm)
- Gold coloured sewing thread to couch on the metallic threads
- Dark green satin 20 cm (8") square
- Red beads 120 x 1 mm (10 for each decoration)

Trace the central scroll and stems of the holly motif on to the centre of 12 of the main pieces of gold satin background fabric, for more information on tracing refer to page 9. *Do not* trace the leaf or berries.

To save time and satin, trace the outline of the holly leaf onto the dark green satin 12 times, cut out a square of bonding web and iron it on the back of the dark green satin behind the leaves. Cut carefully round each leaf, peel off the paper, place the leaf in the correct position on each of the 12 gold satin background squares right side up and iron in place. Place an ironing cloth between the satin and the iron so that the satin is not scorched.

Put the gold satin fabric with backing into a frame then couch the scroll design in place using the craft metallic gold and starting at the tip of the scroll. Fine gold metallic thread is couched around the outside of the leaf, beginning at the

base of the leaf then going down the centre and between the
berries. On the diagram the craft metallic gold is shown with
a solid line and the details, couched with fine gold metallic
thread are shown with a dotted line.

DESIGN TO TRACE

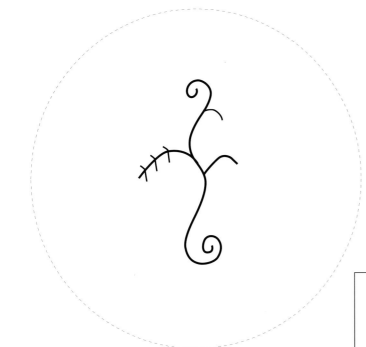

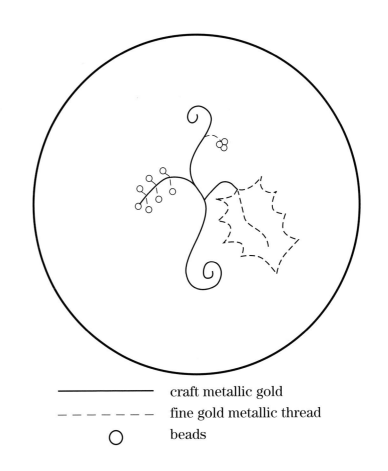

——————————— craft metallic gold

– – – – – – – fine gold metallic thread

◯ beads

> ### HANDY HINT
> You may find it easier to trace the holly leaf
> by the template method

CONSTRUCTION

PREPARATION OF CARDBOARD AND FLANGES

Cut 12 x 9 cm (3 1/2") diameter circles of cardboard to be used as the back of each decoration, smooth the edges with sandpaper. For the front of each decoration I used the plastic flanges as I like the slightly raised shape they have.

Cut 24 x 9cm (3 1/2") in diameter circles of heavy duty vilene to pad the outer side of each cardboard back and the raised side of each flange to be used as the front of each decoration.

Use double sided tape to attach vilene to flanges and cardboard circles

Alternatively if you choose to use cardboard for the front of each decoration, as well as the back, cut 12 more 9 cm (3 1/2") in diameter circles of cardboard and pad them with heavy duty vilene. To create a firm but slightly raised effect for each front, cut from heavy duty vilene, one circle each 9, 7 and 5 cm diameter, (3 1/2", 2 3/4", 2"). When placing the vilene on the cardboard the 5 cm circle is placed on first, the 7 cm circle second and finally the 9 cm circle. (I prefer the firm appearance of vilene to the softer 'spongy' appearance that is obtained with needlepunch - but this is personal.)

ASSEMBLY OF DECORATION

1 Using a sharp sewing needle and a doubled thread of cream sewing cotton, run gathering stitches around the outside of each embroidered back and front making a circle of about 12 cm (4 1/2") diameter. It is best to make the 'gathering' circle bigger than the finished size of the decoration 9 cm (3 1/2") as this leaves you room to accurately centre the design.

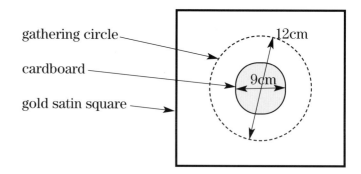

2 Trim the backing fabric and surplus satin back to about 1 cm (1/2") from the gathering stitches.

3   Place cardboard circle (for back) or flange (front) in the centre of the embroidered design making sure that the design is centred on the cardboard/flange with the wrong side of the embroidery resting against the vilene. Pull the gathering thread as tightly as possible. Then work two or three small back stitches in one place to fasten both ends off securely.

4   Check the design is still in the correct position.

5   Lace the design evenly and firmly over the cardboard/flange.

6   Put each completed back and front together making certain that both tops are in line with each other. Place a pin each side and at the bottom to hold the two sides together while you insert the "heavy" gold loop to hang the decoration.

7   Cut a 16 cm (5 1/2") length of "heavy" gold cord, fold in half and leave a 6 cm (2") loop extending beyond the decoration. Tuck the rest of the cord inside between the front and back and stitch very firmly in place at the centre top.

8   Join the front and back of each decoration together by ladder stitching right round the two circles using the cream coloured sewing cotton. Use gold coloured sewing cotton threaded in a Sharp sewing needle to stitch on the 6 mm (1/4") gold metallic braid starting and finishing at the top where the hanging loop is. To make a neat join turn back each end of the braid so that the two folded back edges meet at the hanging loop. (The glue stick helped to hold them in place!)

These decorations would look superb hanging on a tree, decorating the edge of the mantlepiece, or displayed on a wall. They are heirlooms for your home. I do hope you have had as much pleasure making these as I did. May they add magic to Christmas in your home!

Sheila Marshall

OTHER PUBLICATIONS

Exploring Embroidery
- five different techniques with ten different projects published in full colour

THE ELIZABETHAN NEEDLEWORK SERIES

Exploring Elizabethan Embroidery
- the first book in the series - introducing stitches and techniques used in this embroidery with seven different projects to embroider

Elizabethan Needlework Accessories
- the second book in the series - introducing further stitches and techniques with more projects on a needlework theme to embroider

Festive Elizabethan Creations
- the third book in the series - exquisite Elizabethan embroidery for the special occasions in your life

An Elizabethan Christmas
- beautiful Christmas decorations inspired by the life and times of the Elizabethans

OTHER PUBLICATIONS

Time for Beads
- A fascinating introduction to a variety of hand-held beading projects. Your chance to use some of the beautiful beads which are now available.

From My Hands
- Introducing exquisite counted satin stitch and pulled thread designs. Elegant and crisp this embroidery is a joy to see and do!

FORTHCOMING TITLES

An Elizabethan Alphabet
- a beautiful and very personal way to use this embroidery

Blue Ribbon Sampler
- a Prizewinning Sampler for you to create

Exploring Wessex Embroidery
- Your chance to explore a colourful, new technique

PLUS MORE EXCITING TITLES

GEORGESON PUBLISHING LIMITED
P.O. Box 100-667, North Shore Mail Centre, New Zealand
Tel: 64 9 410 2079 Fax: 64 9 410 2069
Email: gpl@georgeson.co.nz
Website: www.georgeson.co.nz